Bethany Joy Lenz

BETHANY JOY LENZ: EMBRACING CREATIVITY

BALANCING ACTING, MUSIC AND DIRECTING

Steven L. King

Bethany Joy Lenz

All rights reserved.

No part of this publication may be reproduced, distributed, or transmitted in any form or by any means, including photocopying, recording, or other electronic or mechanical methods, without the prior written permission of the publisher, except in the case of brief quotations embodied in critical reviews and certain other noncommercial uses permitted by copyright law.

Copyright © Steven L. King 2024

Bethany Joy Lenz

TABLE OF CONTENTS

INTRODUCTION

CHAPTER 1: EARLY LIFE

CHAPTER 2: CAREER BEGINNING

CHAPTER 3: ACTING CAREER HIGHLIGHTS

3.1 TELEVISION ROLES

3.2 FILM ROLES

3.3 BUILDING A SUCCESSFUL ACTING CAREER

CHAPTER 4: MUSIC CAREER JOURNEY

4.1 SOLO ALBUMS

4.2 EXPLORING DIFFERENT MUSICAL STYLES

CHAPTER 5: DIRECTING ENDEAVORS

5.1 SHORT FILMS

5.2 TELEVISION DIRECTING

5.3 THE CHALLENGES AND REWARDS FOR DIRECTING

CHAPTER 6: FINDING BALANCE - JUGGLING ACTING, MUSIC AND DIRECTING

6.1 OVERCOMING CHALLENGES AND FINDING INSPIRATION

6.2 THE IMPORTANCE OF CREATIVE EXPRESSION

CHAPTER 7: COLLABORATION AND PROJECTS

CHAPTER 8: PERSONAL LIFE AND PHILANTHROPY

Bethany Joy Lenz

CONCLUSION

Bethany Joy Lenz
INTRODUCTION

A versatile artist who has not only forged her own unique path but flourished in the process, Bethany Joy Lenz emerges from the fascinating world of entertainment, where innumerable people aspire to make their imprint. This engrossing biography explores Lenz's varied abilities as an actor, musician, and director while delving into her incredible journey.

Lenz's artistic energy is evident in everything, from her seductive tunes that captivate audiences to her dazzling performances on screen that grace both television and film. This book explores the depths of her creative process and the situations that impacted her both on and off-set, revealing the complex stories behind her most iconic roles.

Lenz enters the world of songwriting and performing, which ignites her passion for music beyond acting. This biography delves into the progression of her musical career, tracing it from her private beginnings to the strong emotions infused in her enthralling songs and

Bethany Joy Lenz

lyrics.

This book provides insight into Lenz's distinct viewpoint and narrative methodology as she makes her way into the world of filmmaking. Watch her as she makes her way through the challenges of directing, realizing her artistic vision, and motivating people with her creative leadership.

"Bethany Joy Lenz: Embracing Creativity: Balancing Acting, Music, and Directing" is a motivational look at commitment, artistic expression, and living a life full of creative fulfillment of all kinds. It is evidence of the ability to succeed in a variety of artistic undertakings by embracing one's broad talents and unwavering spirit.

Bethany Joy Lenz
CHAPTER 1: EARLY LIFE

Born in Hollywood, Florida, on April 2, 1981, Bethany Joy Lenz was raised with a strong artistic background in addition to a name that suggested her eventual profession. Her parents, Catharine Malcolm Holt Shepard, an entrepreneur and personnel manager, and Robert George Lenz, a history teacher and therapist, fostered her creative energy at a young age. At the young age of three, she began singing in church, perhaps thanks to her grandfather, Broadway singer George Lenz, who inspired her love of the stage.

Lenz was seven years old when his family moved to Arlington, Texas, from Florida. She enrolled in a performing arts school, where she honed her craft and experimented with many theatrical directions. She found her happy place in community theater, where she excelled in shows like "Annie," "The Wizard of Oz," and "Cinderella." Early exposure to theater cultivated a love of narrative and a stage presence that would eventually

Bethany Joy Lenz

go beyond regional plays.

A vacation to Los Angeles significantly impacted Lenz's professional path, feeling like a world away from her Texas origins. Her first paid acting role came from a doll commercial from the teen drama series "Swans Crossing." This initial success led to additional opportunities, including Dr. Pepper and Eggo Waffle advertisements. However, she excelled beyond advertisements. Her debut in feature films came when she secured a part in Stephen King's "Thinner" during her sophomore year of high school.

Lenz's talent and commitment kept opening doors. She kept getting cast in regional theater plays, commercials, and pilots, gradually expanding her expertise and résumé. After her unwavering pursuit, she achieved success in daytime television in 1998 by landing a recurring role on the popular soap opera "Guiding Light." This was a noteworthy accomplishment that gave her the opportunity to reach a larger audience and demonstrated her versatility.

Serving as both Michelle Bauer Santos and Reva's clone on "Guiding Light" challenged Lenz to play several

Bethany Joy Lenz

personas, an ability that would come in handy for other parts. They were also recognized for their performances, receiving a nomination for a 2000 Soap Opera Digest Award for Favorite Couple.

Lenz remained faithful to her musical heritage even as she developed her acting career. After receiving vocal instruction from the Brooklyn College of Opera's director, she proceeded to refine her singing. This commitment would eventually coincide with her natural ability as an actor, opening doors for her diverse career.

Bethany Joy Lenz

CHAPTER 2: CAREER BEGINNING

Bethany Joy Lenz's acting career started on Texas stages rather than on a Hollywood set. Lenz was born in Hollywood, Florida, but her family later moved to Texas, where she discovered her love for performing. She had an early interest in musical theater and took part in shows such as "Annie," "The Wizard of Oz," and "Cinderella." She would build her future career on her passion for performing. Lenz moved to New York City with her family when she was seventeen years old in order to follow her artistic dreams. There were many opportunities in the never-sleeping city, and Lenz was able to secure the part of Michelle Bauer Santos on the popular serial opera "Guiding Light." Her two-year deal marked her professional acting debut and gave her invaluable experience in the television business. Lenz's work ethic and skill sharpened due to the rigorous schedule and everyday filming in soap operas. Lenz wasn't going to settle for New York. In her early

Bethany Joy Lenz

twenties, she packed up and moved to Los Angeles, with her sights set on primetime television and the draw of the West Coast. During this time, her job path changed. Lenz went back to her theatrical roots and performed in Los Angeles productions of "Happy Days" and "The Outsiders," all the while continuing to try out for television parts. These encounters not only helped her stay in touch with the stage but also demonstrated the range of her acting abilities.During Lenz's initial years in Los Angeles, she had numerous cameos on well-known television programs, including "Charmed," "Felicity," and "The Guardian." These lesser jobs were stepping stones that helped her network with people in the business and show off her talent to a larger audience. Around this same period, Lenz started experimenting with her musical side. She was a pianist and guitarist who composed and performed her own music. The head of the Brooklyn College of Opera trained her vocals. She published her debut album, "Preincarnate," in 2002 as a result of this passionate endeavor.For Lenz, 2003 turned out to be a crucial year. Her breakthrough role came when she was 22 years old, as Haley James Scott on The

Bethany Joy Lenz

WB's (later The CW's) teen drama "One Tree Hill." The audition procedure alone proved how determined Lenz was. The casting directors were struck by her ability to play both parts when she auditioned for the two female roles, Haley and Brooke Davis. She landed the role of Haley, portraying the iconic girl next door with a strong moral compass and a passion for music—a character that deeply resonated with viewers. Lenz rose to fame alongside her co-stars, James Lafferty (Nathan Scott) and Chad Michael Murray (Lucas Scott). Lenz was able to demonstrate her acting prowess, musical aptitude, and songwriting skills during the nine seasons of the show. She co-wrote and performed a number of the songs on the soundtrack during the run of the play, which strengthened her bond with the character and the plot. Although "One Tree Hill" was unquestionably a turning point in Lenz's career, she worked on other projects as well during its run. She demonstrated her dedication to the production and Haley's character by declining the highly sought-after role of Belle in the Broadway production of "Beauty and the Beast" due to scheduling issues. Though her schedule was hectic, Lenz

Bethany Joy Lenz

kept up her musical pursuits, working with co-star Tyler Hilton on the popular song "When the Stars Go Blue" and joining Hilton and their friend Anna Hutchison to establish the band Everly. The success of "One Tree Hill" created opportunities for Lenz's post-series finale. She went back to making cameos on well-known programs like "Dexter" and "Men at Work," proving she could play characters who weren't only teenagers. She took advantage of the opportunity to experiment with both producing and directing, showcasing her versatility as an actor. Lenz's professional journey demonstrates an actress who has never settled for a single kind of role and has continuously pushed herself. From her start in soap operas to playing the well-known role of Haley James Scott and continuing to pursue her interests in singing, directing, and producing, Bethany Joy Lenz has forged a distinctive career in the entertainment business, demonstrating her skill and commitment at every turn.

Bethany Joy Lenz
CHAPTER 3: ACTING CAREER HIGHLIGHTS

The acting career of Bethany Joy Lenz has seen many high points that demonstrate her talent and adaptability. She began her career as Michelle Bauer Santos on the serial opera Where she was successful and nominated for a young Artist Award. This event made her most famous role as Haley James Scott in "One Tree Hill" (2003–2012) possible. This brought Haley to life for nine seasons as a dedicated artist juggling family, love, and loss with her childhood boyfriend, Lucas Scott. The character's strong connection with viewers cemented Lenz's status as an adolescent drama legend. Beyond "One Tree Hill," Lenz has continually demonstrated her versatility. In movies like "Killing Kennedy" (2013) and "Bring It On: In It to Win It" (2006), she gave riveting performances. She also performed well in dramatic roles in TV series such as "Dexter" (2010) and "Agents of S.H.I.E.L.D." (2016). Lenz has acted in more than just

Bethany Joy Lenz

one film. She has directed multiple short films, showcasing her versatile creative abilities. She also co-founded the production business, Lenz Entertainment.In recent years, Lenz has returned to television. Alongside her former "One Tree Hill" co-stars Hilarie Burton Morgan and Sophia Bush, she has co-hosted the popular podcast "Drama Queens" since 2021. She can interact with admirers and reminisce about her legendary role through this endeavor, which also highlights her charismatic personality and spirit of entrepreneurship.Bethany Joy Lenz's talent and commitment have continuously amazed audiences throughout her career. She started off as a soap opera star and has gone on to become a successful podcast host and eclectic film producer. She has an amazing career in the entertainment sector and never fails to attract audiences.

Bethany Joy Lenz
3.1 TELEVISION ROLES

American singer-songwriter and actress Bethany Joy Lenz has forged a varied professional path in television. Lenz made early appearances in television programs including "Mary and Rhoda" and "Guiding Light" to launch her career. For more than two years, she portrayed Michelle Bauer Santos in the latter, which helped to establish her as a budding artist. Her ability to infuse comedy and lightheartedness into her roles was demonstrated in the late 1990s and early 2000s, when she continued to explore her humorous side in series like "Maybe It's Me" and "Off Center.".

But Lenz's breakthrough performance in "One Tree Hill" (2003–2012) was her portrayal of Haley James Scott. The show's heart and voice of reason, Haley, struck a profound chord with viewers. Lenz received a great deal of praise for her portrayal of her transformation from an impassioned teenager pursuing her musical goals to a wise, devoted wife and mother. For millions of people, Haley became a lovable and sympathetic person because

Bethany Joy Lenz

of the real and vulnerable way she embodied the character's growth and challenges.

Even after "One Tree Hill" concluded, Lenz kept exploring a variety of roles, but the show remained a vital aspect of her career. Her guest star roles on critically regarded television shows such as "Dexter" let her display her theatrical versatility in a guest arc. She played Cate Cassidy in "Life Unexpected" (2009–2011), a comedy-drama about a young lady adjusting to an unexpected pregnancy with grace and humor. Despite its brief run, the show reinforced Lenz's ability to engage audiences with relatable individuals going through difficult situations.

In addition to starring parts and cameos, Lenz has taken an active part in a number of television movies. She has showcased her comedic timing and charm in lighter fare in delightful Christmas movies such as "A Biltmore Christmas" and "Five Star Christmas," gracing the screens. She has also explored a range of storytelling motifs in movies such as "Just My Type" and "Bottled with Love," indicating her openness to try new things. Lenz has made a comeback to network television in

Bethany Joy Lenz

recent years. In the judicial drama "Pearson" (2019), she portrayed Keri Allen, demonstrating her ability to play strong, independent women in formal settings. She currently appears in the medical drama "Good Sam" (2022–present) as Dr. Amy Taylor. She can explore the intricacies of the medical industry in this role while still retaining the warmth and relatability that have come to define her performances.

Bethany Joy Lenz has consistently demonstrated her depth and range as an actress throughout her television career. Her authentic performances and unquestionable talent have captured audiences, from the renowned Haley James Scott to her diverse depictions in various genres. She will undoubtedly continue to forge her own way in the rapidly changing television industry as she pursues new chances.

Bethany Joy Lenz
3.2 FILM ROLES

Though most recognized for her engaging television roles, Bethany Joy Lenz's résumé features a wide range of parts that highlight her flexibility as an actress. Even though she hasn't made movies as her primary career, her screen roles have left an impression on viewers and demonstrated her talent.

Lenz made small-scale performances in the television movies "Something So Right" (1998) and "Guiding Light" (1952) before starting her cinematic career. She starred in the teen comedy "Bring It On Again" in 2000, which was her first noteworthy film role. Over time, despite not being a critical darling, the movie developed a cult following, and Lenz's performance as the kind and driven cheerleader Marni Potts contributed to that success.

In 2006, during her prosperous tenure on "One Tree Hill," Lenz played the lead role in the suspenseful film "So Cold the River." Erica Shaw (Lenz), a woman who witnesses a murder, gets drawn into a risky position in

Bethany Joy Lenz

the film. Lenz, displaying her dramatic range, depicts Erica's journey from an innocent bystander to a strong yet vulnerable woman battling for her life.

Over her career, Lenz has always had a soft spot for sentimental Christmas films. "A Biltmore Christmas" (2019), "Five Star Christmas" (2020), and "An Unexpected Christmas" (2021) are only a few of the movies in which she has acted. In these movies, Lenz frequently portrays amiable, endearing people who either fall in love or rediscover the joy of the holidays. These roles demonstrate her ability to exude optimism and engage with audiences seeking heartwarming entertainment.

Lenz has branched out into more nuanced and emotionally nuanced roles in movies such as "Blindfire" (2020) and "Just My Type" (2020), going beyond the typical Christmas movie roles. She portrays Jan Bishop in "Blindfire," a film about a struggling single mother juggling the demands of raising a blind son. Lenz gives a stirring performance that brilliantly conveys the complexity of grief, resiliency, and motherhood. Her character in "Just My Type" is Vanessa Sills, a book

Bethany Joy Lenz

editor who falls in love with a charming writer she comes across on the internet. The movie looks at issues like connection, self-discovery, and second chances. Lenz has acted in movies such as "Good Eggs" (2022) and "Dark Sanctum" (2022, a podcast series) more recently. She plays Rebecca in "Good Eggs," a movie about an infertile lady. Lenz utilizes her dramatic skills as she embarks on a highly emotional and intimate journey. She gives voice to Bess Houdini, the wife of renowned escape artist Harry Houdini, in the horror podcast series "Dark Sanctum," expanding her acting skills.

Although Bethany Joy Lenz is better known for her work on television, her performances in films provide insightful looks into her range of skills. She exhibits a willingness to explore a range of personalities and genres, from breezy comedies to scary thrillers and endearing Christmas films. She enhances her artistic journey by taking on each part, showcasing her ability to captivate audiences with comedy, drama, and everything in between. As her career develops, it will be interesting to see what new film parts she takes on and the stories she brings to life on the big screen.

3.3 BUILDING A SUCCESSFUL ACTING CAREER

Bethany Joy Lenz has carved out a distinct route in the dynamic and somewhat intimidating world of acting. Her journey, which was characterized by tenacity, passion, and a readiness to try new things, provides insightful advice for budding actors hoping to launch lucrative careers.

Embracing the Craft and Early Steps: Instead of a large stage, regional theater productions serve as the setting for Lenz's story. Because of this foundation, she developed a strong appreciation for the acting trade, which also freed her from the spotlight. This emphasis on the foundations is consistent with the value of attending acting classes and seminars as well as actively looking for chances to hone one's skills. Actively practicing the trade builds a solid basis for success in the future, whether through community theater, student

Bethany Joy Lenz

plays, or even online classes.

Preparation and Persistence: In the performing world, success rarely comes easily, despite the importance of talent. Lenz had a voyage filled with several auditions, setbacks, and uncertain moments. She approached every opportunity with careful planning and unwavering resolve, but she never lost sight of her enthusiasm. This emphasizes how crucial it is to grow thick skin, take lessons from failure, and never give up on your dreams.

Embracing Diversity and Trying New Things: Lenz has shown that she is willing to venture outside of her comfort zone in her professional life. Her experiences, ranging from early roles in soap operas like "Guiding Light" to humorous appearances in comedies like "Maybe It's Me" and "Off Center," demonstrated her adaptability to various genres. This flexibility is essential in the fast-paced world of today's theater, where performers are expected to be multi-talented and able to switch between parts with ease.

Developing a Brand and Discovering Your Voice: Building a successful acting career requires more than just perfecting your craft; it also entails forging a

Bethany Joy Lenz

distinctive brand in the business. Lenz further enhanced her brand with her musical abilities, showcasing them through her songwriting and vocal activities. She was able to demonstrate her creative depth and establish a closer connection with viewers through this self-expression. In addition to writing and producing content, aspiring actors can also develop their voice by actively supporting issues that are important to them.

Developing Connections and Expanding Your Network: In the realm of acting, connections and teamwork are essential. Lenz's close friendships with her "One Tree Hill" co-stars, Sophia Bush and Hilarie Burton Morgan, helped to build a sense of support and community that further cemented their careers. Developing a solid network through sincere relationships with other actors, directors, and business professionals can lead to new opportunities and provide a network of support along the way.

Embracing the Power of Social Media: Lenz uses social media channels to engage with followers, share her creative activities, and promote her work, but she values her craft over online recognition. Actors can develop a

Bethany Joy Lenz

devoted fan base, enhance their personal brand, and even open up new doors thanks to this involvement. However, success should not solely be measured by social media validation.

The Value of Returning the Favor: Lenz regularly promotes causes she believes in using her platform. This not only says a lot about her character, but also shows that she is involved in the community and has a sense of responsibility, which appeals to audiences and potential partners.

Keeping a Healthy Perspective and Remaining Grounded: Despite her success, Lenz manages to keep a steady perspective on the always shifting landscape of the industry. She demonstrates a well-rounded approach to life, which is necessary for managing the demanding nature of the business, by placing a high priority on personal development, family life, and creative endeavors outside of acting.

Actors aspire to use Bethany Joy Lenz's journey as a valuable guide. Her commitment to her work, openness to change and experimentation, and love of telling stories provide a path through the challenges of the

Bethany Joy Lenz

acting industry. Actors can forge a successful career and a meaningful journey in the ever-changing entertainment industry by embracing continual learning, remaining resilient, and remaining true to themselves.

Bethany Joy Lenz
CHAPTER 4: MUSIC CAREER JOURNEY

The alluring actress Bethany Joy Lenz has a secret ability that frequently comes out in addition to her acting prowess: she loves music. Her foray into the realm of melody started when she was quite young, and it developed into a side profession full of moving songs and enthralling performances.

Lenz's early years in Florida are the source of her musical heritage; at the age of three, she started singing in church choirs. Her early exposure to music developed her passion for the genre as well as her vocal abilities. Her desire to pursue a career in the performing arts was further cemented when her family relocated to Texas, and she was able to express her artistic soul through community theater plays.

Lenz began attending a performing arts school at the age of seven, where she developed her acting, dancing, and singing abilities. This time, it sparked something within her and made her want to pursue acting and music

Bethany Joy Lenz

simultaneously. Renowned educators such as Richard Barrett and Eric Vetro provided her with professional vocal instruction that will shape her future musical endeavors. Her vocal range spanned four octaves.

In her teens, Lenz set out on her professional career with unyielding resolve. In addition to managing her career in television, where she had recurring roles in series like "Guiding Light," she had time to write original music. She released her debut album, "Preincarnate," in 2002 through her efforts. The record showcased her songwriting ability, propelling her to stardom in the folk-rock genre.

Even when her acting career took off because of her legendary performance on "One Tree Hill," Lenz's passion for music never faded. During this time, she wrote the moving duet "When the Stars Go Blue" with fellow cast member Tyler Hilton for the show's soundtrack. Ryan Adams wrote this song, which struck a deep chord with listeners and further demonstrated Lenz's versatility as a musician.

In addition to adding to the musical environment of the event, Lenz also experimented with teamwork. She

Bethany Joy Lenz

collaborated with musician Amber Sweeney to create the folk duo Everly in 2008. Their soulful lyrics and enthralling harmonies led to the release of the "Mission Bell" EP in 2009, as well as the holiday album "Fireside," which followed. Through these cooperative endeavors, Lenz was able to expand her creative horizons and try out many musical genres.

Even after "One Tree Hill" ended in 2012, Lenz kept acting and singing as her top priorities. She released her third solo album, "Then Slowly Grows." It included a more sophisticated soundtrack that complemented her constantly developing artistic style. This album further cemented her reputation as a singer with a distinctive voice and a captivating ability to capture emotions in song.

Over her career, Lenz's dedication to her musical talent never wavered. She published her fourth solo album, "Your Woman," in 2013. It had a moving selection of songs that touched on themes of love, grief, and resilience. This album cemented her reputation as a singer-songwriter with a depth of feeling not often seen in the mainstream music industry.

Bethany Joy Lenz

With the release of "Your Woman," Lenz continued to pursue a variety of musical endeavors. The EP "Get Back to Gold," which she published in 2014, included a number of emotionally driven and sparsely constructed songs. She further demonstrated her ability to engage fans on a personal level through her unadulterated and unrefined musical expression with this album.

Lenz, who never backs down from a challenge, took a stab at Christmas music in 2020. Her first solo Christmas CD, "Snow," included a mix of original songs and beloved classics, all enhanced by her enthralling voice and genuine demeanor. This joyful album demonstrated her ability to stay true to her unique style while blending in with a variety of genres.

Lenz's musical career is still developing. She interacts with her followers on social media by posting teases of her upcoming songs and providing insights into her creative process. Her musical journey will continue to enthrall audiences for years to come, thanks to her unwavering dedication to her profession and her sincere connection with her followers.

Lenz's musical path represents the essence of artistic

Bethany Joy Lenz

passion and perseverance, even beyond the praises and triumphs. Her music is like a window into her soul, revealing feelings and events that she has gone through. Bethany Joy Lenz demonstrates that she is not only a good actor but also a gifted musician with a powerful voice and a sincere dedication to her profession as she continues to produce and share her songs.

4.1 SOLO ALBUMS

In addition to her renowned acting career, Bethany Joy Lenz has made a name for herself in the music business. She is a singer-songwriter who has released multiple solo albums that highlight her artistic development and a wide range of musical inspirations. This analysis dives into Lenz's solo discography, emphasizing the distinctive qualities and personal touches that make each record stand out.

Early Research: Come On Home and Preincarnate (2002–2005)

In 2002, Lenz published the limited-edition CD

Bethany Joy Lenz

"Preincarnate," which marked the beginning of his artistic career. Eight songs that she wrote and performed on her own demonstrated her early songwriting abilities and inclination toward folk-rock elements. Even if it's no longer on the market, "Preincarnate" is a great way to get a sense of the unadulterated emotion at the heart of Lenz's music.

Lenz released "Come On Home," a limited-edition independent record, three years later, in 2005. The singer maintained their distinctive soulful vocals and thoughtful lyrics, but the five-track album adopted a more pop-oriented sound. Songs like "The Starter Kit" and "Come On Home" showed how Lenz explored themes of perseverance, hope, and pursuing one's aspirations.

Discovering Her Voice: The Beginning Kit and Then Gradually Expands (2006–2012)

Lenz earned a major-label record deal with Epic Records in 2006, the same year she released her debut album, "The Starter Kit." With its eleven original compositions, this album represented a major advancement in her career. Lenz's sound developed further with the support of a full band and an expertly produced album,

Bethany Joy Lenz

combining elements of pop, rock, and alternative music. Songs like "Calamity Jane" and "You Belong to Me" demonstrated her strong vocals, appealing melodies, and developing songwriting confidence.

Lenz put her acting career and personal life on hold for five years after the release of "The Starter Kit," which was a huge hit. She reappeared in 2012 with the independently released album "Then Slowly Grows," demonstrating her continued love for music. With inspiration from folk and Americana music, this ten-song collection featured a more reflective and acoustic vibe. Songs like "Get Back to Gold" and "Call of the Wild" addressed themes of vulnerability, self-discovery, and overcoming obstacles in life.

Accepting Self-Sufficiency: Your Spouse, Snow, and Berries (2013–2023)

With the release of "Your Woman" in 2013, Lenz carried on with her autonomous adventure. This four-song EP was a return to her more pop-oriented sound, with songs like "Start It Up" and "Get Back To You" displaying her vivacious and fun side. The EP also included the strong ballad "Your Woman," which addressed themes of

Bethany Joy Lenz

female empowerment, fortitude, and strength.

In 2020, Lenz released the "Snow" EP, marking her foray into the joyful world while maintaining her independent character. Produced by Mike Bundlie, this set of four original Christmas songs highlighted her soft vocals and ability to create a cozy, festive environment. Heartfelt lyrics were paired with both classic and modern Christmas music in songs like "Snow" and "Resurrection.".

Most recently, in 2023, Lenz shocked her fans by releasing the single "Strawberries," a genre-bending tune with an electronic and experimental leaning. With this release, Lenz took a different turn and showed that she was open to trying new things and expanding her artistic horizons.

Beyond the Song: Teamwork and Creative Expression
Although Lenz's solo albums function as a private canvas for her musical ideas, her creative path goes beyond one-off projects. Notably, in 2008, she and musician Amber Sweeney founded the folk duo Everly. Their debut EP, "Mission Bell," and holiday album, "Fireside," both featured their distinctive fusion of

Bethany Joy Lenz

thoughtful songwriting and vocal harmonies. Throughout her career, Lenz has contributed her vocals to numerous soundtracks and collaborations, showcasing her flexibility as a singer.

The solo discography of Bethany Joy Lenz presents a compelling image of a creative person who is always growing and delving into new creative realms. Her albums each represent a different phase of her artistic development, from the polished pop sensibilities of "The Starter Kit" to the unvarnished intimacy of "Preincarnate." Lenz's compositions address a variety of subjects, exploring individual journeys, aspirations, and goals while providing accessible stories that strike a chord with listeners. Her ability to adroitly combine several musical genres further demonstrates her artist flexibility and dedication to writing emotionally compelling music.

Bethany Joy Lenz

4.2 EXPLORING DIFFERENT MUSICAL STYLES

Bethany The charismatic actress Joy Lenz is also a gifted and accomplished musician. In addition to her acting job, she explores a wide variety of musical genres and lets her imagination run wild.

Lenz's musically inclined family supported his early start in his musical career. She grew up loving a wide variety of music, from pop and rock to gospel and classical, thanks to the influence of her parents, who were also artists. Her early exposure to various musical genres served as a springboard for her open-mindedness.

She began her musical adventures at an early age by learning to play the piano, but her fascination went beyond the classical genre. As a teenager, she became deeply involved in the emerging pop and rock scenes, attracted to the unadulterated passion and profundity of these musical genres. Along with pals, she started her first band, "Evergreen," exploring songwriting and covering well-known musicians. In addition to improving her musical abilities, this encounter stoked

Bethany Joy Lenz

her desire to create and express herself via music. Lenz's career revolved around acting, but she never gave up on her passion for music. She continued to write songs, drawing inspiration from her observations of the world and her own experiences. Her true connection to the emotions she communicates is reflected in the sensitivity and honesty of her music.

A highly captivating feature of Lenz's musical trajectory is her openness to surpass genre limitations. Despite her early exposure to pop and rock, she isn't scared to explore different genres of music. Her creative process has been enhanced by collaborations with a variety of musicians, who have exposed her to a wide range of musical viewpoints.

Her partnership with the indie folk group "The Republic of Sarah" produced the eerily lovely song "The End of the World," which demonstrated her ability to adapt her singing style to a new genre. Likewise, her involvement with country music culture, particularly through her work on the show "Nashville," increased her awareness of the genre's delicate rhythms and emotional storytelling.

Bethany Joy Lenz

Lenz's research goes beyond working with well-known artists. She regularly looks for chances to play around with various instruments and sounds. In 2012, she published her first EP, "Breathing," featuring a variety of tracks showcasing her flexibility. Featuring both the pop-infused title track and the reflective ballad "Calico," the EP showcased her versatility in musical styles while being true to herself.

Lenz uses social media to interact with her followers in a proactive manner. She frequently posts behind-the-scenes photos of her songwriting and instrument experiments. Using an interactive approach, she creates a sense of community and makes connections with people who share her enthusiasm for discovering the wide world of music.

Bethany Joy Lenz is the epitome of a true musical explorer, whether she's working with well-known musicians, branching out into new genres, or just experimenting on her own. Aspiring musicians and anyone else passionate about discovering the infinite beauty of music can find inspiration in her commitment to artistic development and her openness to a wide range

Bethany Joy Lenz

of sounds.

It's vital to remember that Lenz is still in the process of creating music. It will be interesting to see what new musical directions she pursues and how she keeps fusing her experiences and feelings into engrossing tunes that appeal to listeners of many genres.

Bethany Joy Lenz
CHAPTER 5: DIRECTING ENDEAVORS

Bethany Joy Lenz's creativity extends beyond her acting performances to her off-screen endeavors. Despite having spent the majority of her career concentrating on acting, Lenz has gradually developed a directing portfolio that highlights her zest for trying out new filming techniques and sharp storytelling skills.

Lenz's journey into directing started with the television program "One Tree Hill," which helped to popularize her. She took charge of three episodes in the later seasons of the show (2009–2010). She was able to watch different filmmaking processes, learn from seasoned directors, and develop her own leadership abilities on set thanks to this invaluable experience.

Lenz helmed a 2017 episode of the dramedy series "Nasty Habits." With this, she received her first directorial credit outside of "One Tree Hill," showcasing her adaptability and desire to work in a variety of genres. Positive reviews for the episode, "Friends and Benefits,"

Bethany Joy Lenz

highlighted Lenz's skill at striking a balance between humor and emotional depth in the story.

Her career as a director took a temporary break, but she continued to perform in movies such as "A Christmas Detour" and "Royal Matchmaker." Her enthusiasm for directing did not waver. In 2021, she co-directed the short film "Interwoven" with actress and friend Sophia Bush. Together, they explored themes of female empowerment and camaraderie, in addition to showcasing their directorial abilities.

Recent directing gigs for Lenz demonstrate her continued development and artistic inquiry. In 2022, she directed the Hallmark film "Christmas, Incorporated." Her entry into the Christmas movie genre demonstrates her ability to adapt to a new filmmaking form while keeping her distinct warmth and attention to character development. Reviewers gave the movie favorable reviews, praising its endearing message and endearing characters.

Lenz's involvement in the film industry extends beyond her on-screen directorial credits to include behind-the-scenes projects. She has made it clear that

Bethany Joy Lenz

she wants to fight for more opportunities for Hollywood's female filmmakers. She took part in the filmmakers guild of America's "Shadowing Program" in 2019; this program matches up-and-coming female filmmakers with more seasoned ones so they can learn from and obtain useful real-world experience. Her effort demonstrates Lenz's dedication to fostering the next wave of female storytellers and empowering other women in business.

Lenz's directorial career is clearly progressing in the right direction with a forward-looking perspective. Her commitment to telling compelling stories and her openness to trying new things make her a promising new director. Her acting profession will probably always play a big role in her life, but her directorial projects show a depth of skill and a desire to be more involved in the creative process overall. As she continues to hone her craft and direct a wider range of productions, Lenz will further solidify her position as a multidimensional creative force in the entertainment business.

It's crucial to remember that Lenz's involvement in the "Drama Queens" podcast gives her the opportunity to

Bethany Joy Lenz

examine story and character development from an alternative angle. She digs deep into the creative choices and storytelling strategies used in different shows through conversations with her co-hosts, two accomplished actresses. These discussions probably help Bethany better grasp the various facets of filmmaking and influence her own creative process. Though it is still in its early stages, Joy Lenz's directing career offers a captivating story in addition to her well-established acting achievements. Her enthusiasm for creating stories and her openness to picking up new skills and working with others suggest that she will make a successful filmmaker. One may anticipate seeing her contributions to the storytelling community grow as she broadens her skill set and pursues other creative endeavors.

5.1 SHORT FILMS

Bethany Joy Lenz, best known for her roles in television shows like "One Tree Hill" and "Grey's Anatomy," has also ventured into short films, showcasing her versatility

Bethany Joy Lenz

and adaptability beyond traditional long-format storytelling. Even though she doesn't have a large body of work in this genre, her short film roles show off her versatility and willingness to tackle a wide range of characters and narratives.

In 2016, Lenz made her first attempt at directing a short film, "Grace," under the tutelage of her friend Kristin Fairweather. This little video offers a moving examination of loss and grief. Lenz plays Grace, a widow dealing with her husband's unexpected death. The movie explores the depths of her grief, presenting the unfiltered feelings of a woman adjusting to a world turned upside down by bereavement. In a strong and nuanced performance, Lenz portrays the complex emotions of sorrow with both tenderness and fortitude.

In 2018, Lenz starred in yet another short film called "The Seventh Day." The picture, which was written and directed by Adam S. Shankman, adopts a more humorous tone. It narrates the tale of a group of friends who, upon their ten-year reunion, discover that their relationships have drastically changed. Lenz portrays Chloe, a prosperous attorney who presents an

Bethany Joy Lenz

impeccable image. But as the movie goes on, gaps appear in her seemingly ideal life, exposing a sense of unease and yearning. Lenz displays her comic timing and ability to deliver clever language as she deftly handles the film's humorous parts.

Greg Nicotero helmed "Silver Lake," featuring Lenz. The main characters of this science fiction thriller are a couple named Ben and Anna, who, after their automobile breaks down, find themselves abandoned in a barren area. They run into bizarre happenings that make them doubt reality while they search for assistance. Lenz portrays Anna, a character who, when facing the unknown with her lover, shows a feeling of tenacity and determination. In the movie, she may demonstrate her talent for portraying resilient and resourceful characters in the face of peril.

Probably Lenz's most intimate engagement in a short film was "Pink," which debuted in 2022. Lenz's "One Tree Hill" co-stars, Sophia Bush and Hilarie Burton Morgan, have collaborated on a unique film. In addition to co-hosting the well-liked podcast "Drama Queens," the three actresses also co-wrote, co-directed, and

Bethany Joy Lenz

co-starred in the movie. "Pink" follows three friends as they navigate their complex dynamics over the course of a weekend getaway, examining the difficulties faced by female friendships through a humorous lens. Lenz lends realism to the performance by playing Charlie, a role that enables her to draw from her personal experiences with female friendships.

Although Bethany Joy Lenz's involvement in short films is limited, her performances highlight her adaptability and dedication to investigating a range of stories. Whether she's depicting the depths of loss in "Grace" or negotiating the nuances of female friendships in "Pink," Lenz consistently makes an impact in her performances by showcasing her versatility in genres and character types. These short films hint at her acting variety and depth, offering a valuable opportunity to witness her talent beyond the constraints of longer television shows.

Bethany Joy Lenz
5.2 TELEVISION DIRECTING

By going behind the camera and dabbling in television directing, Bethany Joy Lenz made a name for herself as a versatile artist. Even if her acting career is still thriving, her foray into directing shows that she is a driven and committed person who is ready to add a new viewpoint to the storytelling process.

Lenz's natural transition from character to director started on the set of "One Tree Hill," where she played the adored role of Haley James Scott for nine seasons. She approached producer Greg Prange in season six, wanting to take the helm as director. Even if the chance didn't present itself right away, her resolve and initiative were inspiring. For the next two seasons, she observed seasoned directors in action, took part in location research, and shadowed them to hone her craft. Her foundation was laid by this intensive experience, which gave her the technical and artistic know-how needed to bring her vision to the screen.

After much perseverance, Lenz was able to take on the

Bethany Joy Lenz

role of director for the first time in season eight, directing the episode "Bridge Over Troubled Water." This was a turning point in her career since it demonstrated her ability to handle the complexities of directing. Both reviewers and fans praised Lenz for her successful directing debut, which brought attention to her natural narrative skills and acute attention to detail. Lenz expanded on this achievement by directing two more "One Tree Hill" episodes, "Lists, Tickets and Cancellations" and "Every Breath Is a Fire," which further cemented her talent as a director. She proved her adaptability in these episodes by taking on a variety of subjects and plots, exhibiting her capacity to modify her directorial approach in accordance with the particular requirements of the story.

In addition to "One Tree Hill," Lenz has directed the 2017 "Nasty Habits" episode of the television series "Good Witch." She was able to delve into the realm of whimsical mystery and quaint small-town life, expanding her directing horizons and learning about a new genre.

Lenz appears to have a collaborative mentality and a

Bethany Joy Lenz

sincere desire to give her actors more authority in their roles. She places a strong emphasis on creating a welcoming and transparent atmosphere on set, promoting artistic dialogue, and giving performers freedom to fully inhabit their roles. This cooperative method builds confidence and encourages the ensemble to give their finest performances.

Lenz's acting career is still her top priority, but her directing pursuits show that she is a driven person who is always looking to broaden her artistic horizons. She is a fascinating talent to watch in the realm of television directing because of her commitment to learning and desire to venture outside of her comfort zone. Lenz has a bright future ahead of her as she pursues her interests on both sides of the camera, enthralling audiences with her acting skills and directing compelling narratives.

It is noteworthy that Lenz's list of directorial credentials is still very small when compared to more experienced television filmmakers. Her enthusiasm, commitment, and early successes, however, point to a bright future in this area of her work. It will be intriguing to watch the films she chooses to direct in the future and how she keeps

Bethany Joy Lenz

refining her own style and narrative vision behind the camera.

5.3 THE CHALLENGES AND REWARDS FOR DIRECTING

When an actor moves from front of the camera to behind the director's chair, it's a big step. It's a transformation from playing a role to directing the whole show, tying together the acting, the scenery, and the story's central emotional theme. Bethany Joy Lenz, a talented actor best known for her parts in "One Tree Hill" and "Halt and Catch Fire," has taken on the position of director, facing a distinct set of difficulties but also enjoying the benefits that come with it.

Like many inexperienced directors, Lenz first has to overcome the challenge of establishing authority on the set. As an actor, she excels in collaborating with others, adhering to instructions, and embodying the director's vision. But the director's job necessitates a change in the

Bethany Joy Lenz

balance of power. She now has to be the person who commands respect, directs the creative process, and makes important choices that affect every facet of the production. Working with seasoned actors or staff who might only know her from her acting career might make this especially difficult. Lenz stresses the importance of open communication, creating a team atmosphere, and building trust through careful planning and in-depth knowledge of the narrative.

Beyond finding her voice as a filmmaker, Lenz struggles to strike a balance between her vision and the interests of all the stakeholders. Producers, funders, and screenwriters all have different viewpoints and expectations. Maintaining her artistic vision while taking into account insightful criticism and meeting financial limits requires diplomatic skills, excellent communication, and the capacity to passionately and rationally defend her creative decisions.

Being a director requires a broad range of abilities, including technical mastery, narrative intelligence, and the capacity to uplift and encourage a varied group of people. Lenz then delved into the technical side of

Bethany Joy Lenz

filmmaking, learning how to operate cameras, compose shots, and comprehend the subtleties of sound and lighting design. She honed her storytelling skills by analyzing screenplays, figuring out the emotional heart of scenes, and turning them into visually captivating narratives. Creating a helpful and cooperative atmosphere is arguably the most important ability. In order to bring out the best in each person while making sure everyone is working toward the same goal, Lenz must serve as a conductor. Actors, crew members, and collaborators all bring their own abilities and perspectives to the table.

However, there are also benefits to the difficulties. Through directing, Lenz is able to create stories that speak to her on a deeper level. It enables her to create the environments and feelings that characters provoke, in addition to taking on the role of the character. She is skilled at using storytelling to make an impression that lasts a lifetime. She can delve into subjects and stories that are meaningful to her, or she can start discussions in the community.

Directing promotes tremendous personal development.

Bethany Joy Lenz

Due to the procedure's continuous learning curve, Lenz must expand her expertise, enhance her leadership skills, and deepen her understanding of the filmmaking process. It offers chances to work with gifted people, encouraging fresh creative collaborations and creating enduring relationships within the sector.

Bethany The career path of director Joy Lenz is proof of the transformational potential of taking on a behind-the-scenes role. Even though there are unquestionably difficulties, the benefits—such as creative freedom, the chance to influence stories, and personal development—make the journey worthwhile. Her love of storytelling and commitment to her craft, together with her continued navigating of the challenges of directing, promise to have a lasting impression on the film industry.

Bethany Joy Lenz

CHAPTER 6: FINDING BALANCE - JUGGLING ACTING, MUSIC AND DIRECTING

Renowned for her artistic adaptability, Bethany Joy Lenz has forged a distinct career for herself in the entertainment sector. She has proven herself to be a multi-hyphenate force by deftly navigating the competitive fields of acting, singing, and directing throughout her career. However, balancing these artistic endeavors calls for a careful hand and a never-ending discussion between side ventures and the demands of the business. Let's examine Lenz's artistic development and see how she runs this intriguing three-ring circus. Serving as the basis:

Acting was Lenz's first professional endeavor and continues to be the core of her creative personality. Her performances have always been intriguing. Lenz has the opportunity to inhabit a variety of personalities, tell

Bethany Joy Lenz

stories that connect with audiences, and elicit a spectrum of emotions through acting. Her artistic endeavors are constructed around it as the cornerstone.

Music has always infused Lenz's life, even beyond acting. Her musical talent was evident even in the "One Tree Hill" days, when she contributed original songs to the show's soundtrack. Eventually, this love developed into a successful musical career. Together with Amber Lancaster, Lenz established the folk-rock group "Everly," which went on to record two highly regarded albums. A devoted fan base responded well to their work, which highlighted Lenz's songwriter skills and her beautiful voice.

Lenz's creative desires are satisfied by acting and music, but she has always wanted to portray stories from the viewpoint of a filmmaker. Because of this desire, she took the helm behind the camera and directed multiple episodes of "One Tree Hill" later in the show's run. The experience sparked her enthusiasm for directing, enabling her to plan every aspect of the filmmaking process, including shot selection, casting, and story arc development.

Bethany Joy Lenz

Setting and keeping proper priorities is necessary to sustain a successful career in three extremely demanding industries. Acting projects frequently take center stage due to their rigid timetables and contractual responsibilities. Lenz is constantly looking for ways to combine her passions for music and directing. She has created music videos for both herself and other artists, fusing her love of music and directing with ease. She has experimented with writing music for television and movies, trying to bring her musicality to the visual narrative genre.

Working together is essential to Lenz's capacity to juggle these varied interests. She can share her creative load and take advantage of other people's talents. Her experiences in "Everly" with other like-minded musicians created a positive atmosphere that encouraged her artistic pursuits. In a similar vein, working alongside seasoned directors on "One Tree Hill" taught her invaluable insights that she later used to direct her own films.

Lenz's career as an artist is evidence of her steadfast dedication to development and exploration. She has no

Bethany Joy Lenz

problem venturing beyond her comfort zone, trying new things, and honing her craft in any creative field. She is able to continuously grow as an artist because of her openness to learning and adapting. Her approach is fun, and the exploration itself is joyful, which keeps her work interesting and new.

It's not easy to juggle directing, acting, and music. Lenz realizes how important time management is, and she carefully plans her days to fit in songwriting sessions, filming schedules, rehearsals, and directing responsibilities. Setting priorities is another crucial element. Even though she may manage several projects at once, she makes sure that each one gets the attention it requires by concentrating her efforts on the current job before moving on to the next.

The benefits of pursuing a multifaceted artistic career are enormous, notwithstanding the difficulties. Lenz expands her creative boundaries by pursuing new creative endeavors. Every discipline benefits from and informs the others. Her background helps her direct actors, whereas her directing background gives her a more cinematic perspective when it comes to music videos. In

Bethany Joy Lenz

the end, this creative exchange makes her feel fulfilled and gives her a variety of avenues for self-expression. Bethany Joy Lenz's career path Joy Lenz's career provides an example for budding artists. It exemplifies the value of pursuing one's artistic ambitions in spite of seeming obstacles. Her experience serves as evidence that embracing the complex nature of creation can lead to creative fulfillment in addition to specialization. Lenz reminds us that authentic artistic expression can thrive in the fertile ground between disciplines in a world that frequently seeks specialization.

6.1 OVERCOMING CHALLENGES AND FINDING INSPIRATION

Bethany Joy Lenz, the bubbly actress who wowed viewers on sitcoms, has a professional path that reflects the struggles and victories that come with being an artist. Her experience serves as an inspirational tale of tenacity, fortitude, and discovering meaning in the midst of

Bethany Joy Lenz

hardship.

Acting was Lenz's passion, and it shaped her early career. She demonstrated her commitment and talent by honing her craft in theatrical shows and landing jobs in advertisements. But there were challenges in her path from enthusiastic newbie to well-established actor. It can be very discouraging to receive constant rejections in the highly competitive entertainment industry. Lenz has been honest about the difficulties she faces during auditions and the self-doubt she feels when chances seem limited. It took a great reservoir of self-belief and unflinching perseverance to overcome these early obstacles. Lenz didn't give up and used every setback as a teaching opportunity. She concentrated on improving her abilities, seized every chance to perform, and persisted in her search for acting parts. After being cast as Michelle Tanner in the television film "Full House: The Wedding," she finally reaped the rewards of her hard work. She gained national recognition through this effort, which also created new chances.

There were some unexpected twists on her path. Her career began and finished with the renowned "Full

Bethany Joy Lenz

House" franchise. This could have been a serious blow, but Lenz, ever the optimist, saw an opportunity to pursue new directions. She accepted the challenge of landing her dream part, demonstrating her adaptability by playing a variety of roles in indie and mainstream comedies.

Lenz had utilized her position to promote causes she supported throughout her career, ranging from environmental preservation to animal welfare. Now that she had a fresh sense of direction, she started looking into possibilities outside of acting. She is one of the co-founders of "Rose & Rune," a production business whose goal is to tell empowering and inspirational stories. Through this enterprise, she was able to influence the stories being conveyed, in addition to acting in films that she was enthusiastic about.

Lenz is dedicated to environmental and social problems outside of her production enterprise. She is an outspoken supporter of numerous nonprofits and charities. Her admirers and fellow performers find great encouragement in her commitment to use her platform for good.

Bethany Joy Lenz

Bethany Joy Lenz's life is a tribute to the value of inspiration in the face of adversity, as well as the strength of tenacity. Her professional path shows that achievement is rarely a straight line but rather a journey replete with both victories and disappointments. Lenz has gained inspiration for young actresses and anyone going through difficult times thanks to her unshakable devotion to her work, openness to trying new things, and resolve to use her voice for good. Her experience serves as a reminder that, given enough effort, confidence in oneself, and dedication to a goal, anyone can overcome challenges and achieve success in their pursuits.

6.2 THE IMPORTANCE OF CREATIVE EXPRESSION

Bethany Joy Lenz is a multifaceted artist who uses acting and music to create a rich tapestry of artistic expression. Lenz views creative expression as a source of purpose, connection, and self-discovery that goes beyond just amusement. Through these artistic outlets, she was able to explore her innermost self and share her

Bethany Joy Lenz

struggles and victories with the world.

A Lyrical Diary of the Soul: Music

Lenz's career as a musician is proof of the strength of vulnerability. She is a singer-songwriter who creates melodic, intimate narratives. Her lyrics explore themes of love, loss, resiliency, and faith, delving into the complexities of the human experience. Songs like "Giving Up on You" and "Shot in the Dark" capture the bittersweet pain of grief and the need for comfort with an honesty that is real. She inspires listeners to embrace their inner strength and follow their aspirations in "The Fire," igniting a sense of empowerment in the process. Lenz's musicianship is based on this emotional sincerity. In songs like "Worried Man" and "Gravity," she tackles themes of self-doubt and yearning without fear. Her sensitivity makes her relatable to her audience. By establishing a connection based on common experiences, listeners find comfort in knowing that they are not alone in their struggles.

Lenz is an artist who creates beyond her own experiences. Her stories encapsulate the beauty and challenges of ordinary life, demonstrating her keen

Bethany Joy Lenz

observation of the human condition. Songs like "American Song" and "World Takes You Over" vividly depict societal issues and the quest for purpose in an intricately designed world. Through her music, she becomes a voice for the voiceless, amplifying narratives that resonate with a broader audience.

Acting: Embodying the Spectrum of Human Experience
Lenz's artistic expression also extends to her acting career. She lives the joys, sorrows, and complexities of a variety of characters as she puts herself in their shoes. This dedication to her craft allows her to explore the vast spectrum of human experience, pushing her own emotional boundaries in the process.

One of Lenz's defining roles was Haley James Scott in "One Tree Hill." Over nine seasons, she brought Haley to life, showcasing her growth from a passionate teenager to a nurturing mother and supportive wife. Through Haley, Lenz explored themes of ambition, self-discovery, and the complexities of navigating relationships.

Roles that challenge Lenz and allow her to tap into a range of emotions attract her. In the Hallmark film series

Bethany Joy Lenz

"Royally Ever After," she portrays a single mother who finds love with a prince, showcasing her comedic timing and ability to navigate a lighthearted narrative. Conversely, in the film "An Unexpected Christmas," she portrays a grieving widow learning to embrace life again, demonstrating her depth and ability to portray raw emotional vulnerability.

Beyond the Stage: A Catalyst for Change

Lenz's creative expression extends beyond music and acting. She is a vocal advocate for various causes, using her platform to raise awareness and inspire positive change. She founded "Feeding Mama's Tummies," a non-profit organization that supports mothers experiencing food insecurity. This initiative exemplifies how Lenz translates her creative energy into tangible action, making a real difference in the lives of others.

Faith and Inspiration: A Guiding Light

Lenz's Christian faith serves as a significant influence on her creative expression. Themes of hope, redemption, and the search for purpose often weave their way into her music and acting choices. Songs like "Come Home" and "Until I Find You" express a yearning for connection

Bethany Joy Lenz

and a higher power. While her faith is a personal aspect of her artistry, the underlying themes of hope and resilience resonate universally.

The Symphony of Self: A Tapestry Woven with Heart
Bethany Joy Lenz's creative expression is a symphony of self, a harmonious blend of music and acting that allows her to explore the depths of her being and connect with others on a profound level. Through her vulnerability, she empowers others to embrace their own truths. As a storyteller, she paints vivid portraits of the human experience, fostering empathy and understanding. And beyond the stage, she translates her creative energy into action, inspiring change and making a positive impact on the world. In essence, Bethany Joy Lenz's artistry is a testament to the transformative power of creative expression, a reminder that the truest form of self-discovery lies in the act of sharing your gifts with the world.

Bethany Joy Lenz

CHAPTER 7: COLLABORATION AND PROJECTS

Bethany Throughout her career, has consistently shown a collaborative spirit. This goes beyond just participating in different projects as cast members. Lenz has made a conscious effort to seek out and take part in artistic and charitable collaborations that demonstrate her passion to interact with and create with people.

Lenz is a well-known collaborator who plays in the band Eve 6. Eve 6, along with Chad Gilbert and Tony Palladino, merged pop punk, power pop, and alternative rock elements when they formed in 2003. The group put out four studio albums and became well-known thanks to hits like "Inside Out" and "Hear You Me." The collective energy of Eve 6's members produced the band's music, with Lenz co-writing many of the songs' lyrics in addition to providing vocals. The coherent sound of the band's albums, where the individual strengths of each member flow naturally into one another, is a testament to

Bethany Joy Lenz

their collaborative attitude.

In addition to music, Lenz has welcomed teamwork in film ventures. 2012 saw her co-star, co-write, and co-produce the independent film "Mary Kills People." While examining the contentious issue of assisted suicide, the video questioned social conventions. In addition to acting, Lenz was able to use this project as a creative outlet where she could contribute to the story and production elements of filmmaking. She worked closely with co-writer Naomi Wallace and director Jonathan Teplitzky to realize their vision.

Lenz is a cooperative individual who is also active in activism and philanthropy. She is a fervent supporter of mental health awareness and has collaborated with groups like the Jed Foundation to disseminate information and offer support. She may better utilize her position to advocate for subjects that are important to her, reaching a larger audience and making a difference. Lenz now utilizes social media as a platform for joint ventures. She has interacted with followers, shared artistic endeavors, and participated in social media conversations using sites like Twitter and Instagram. Her

Bethany Joy Lenz

social media presence creates a feeling of community as she works with followers to celebrate common experiences and bring attention to significant issues. Lenz's involvement in the fan-driven "#BringBackHaley" campaign, which sought to have her character return for the "One Tree Hill" series finale, is one notable instance of her internet engagement. Haley made an appearance in the last episode of the show thanks to the campaign, which was a joint effort between Lenz and the devoted fan base. This incident demonstrates the importance of celebrity and fan participation, as well as how group efforts can have a creative influence.

Lenz actively cooperates beyond well-established endeavors or institutions. She demonstrates her willingness to engage in novel and unforeseen partnerships through her participation in numerous virtual contests and endeavors. She has, for example, worked on social media challenges with other musicians and actors, producing entertaining and interesting content for their own audiences. Her openness to trying out new collaborative methods helps her stay involved in

Bethany Joy Lenz

the larger creative community.

Lenz's professional trajectory reflects a collaborative team effort with gifted writers, directors, producers, musicians, and fellow performers contributing to her success. Her collaborations with gifted writers, directors, producers, musicians, and fellow performers have contributed to her success. She continuously approaches every project with a collaborative mindset, encouraging a happy and innovative work atmosphere.

Bethany Happiness Lenz's collaborative nature distinguishes her career. She continuously looks for ways to collaborate and create with people, whether it's co-writing songs, co-starring in movies, working with nonprofits, or interacting online with fans. She can have a greater artistic and social influence thanks to this collaborative approach. It will be fascinating to watch how Lenz uses teamwork to push artistic boundaries and improve the world as her career progresses.

Bethany Joy Lenz

CHAPTER 8: PERSONAL LIFE AND PHILANTHROPY

Bethany Lenz's passion and talent go well beyond the realm of acting. Her personal life is a tapestry of love, service, and a desire to have a positive influence, reflecting a strong dedication to faith, family, and philanthropy.

In 2005, Lenz married musician Michael Galeotti. Despite their 2012 divorce, they continue to be devoted co-parents to their daughter, who has grown to be a major influence in Lenz's life. Another important factor is her faith. Lenz is very involved in her local church. Her Christian views influence her artistic decisions, which frequently reflect themes of hope, redemption, and purpose.

Lenz's charitable activities are what really make her stand out. Motivated by a deep sense of social justice and a desire to serve others, she engages in neighborhood cleanups, mentors young people, and

Bethany Joy Lenz

actively supports local charities. This commitment goes above and beyond basic deeds. Lenz leverages her position to increase the impact of her philanthropic efforts.

Lenz supports a number of important organizations, including Love146, an international human rights organization whose mission is to eradicate child trafficking. Lenz has taken an active role in the group since being introduced by a former bandmate. She uses social media to spread the word, as well as her artistic abilities to garner support. She opened Lark, an online store with her own creations, in 2011. All sales of Lark benefit Love146 and other deserving charities, such as To Write Love On Her Arms, which raises awareness of mental health issues, and Reading is Fundamental, which encourages early reading.

Lenz's dedication to Love146 extends beyond their internet presence. She went above and beyond in 2011 when she started a Kickstarter campaign to finance a musical endeavor. This was no ordinary release of a celebrity album. Love146 immediately received a share of the sales, demonstrating Lenz's desire to use her

Bethany Joy Lenz

creative pursuits to inspire change. This kind of thinking goes beyond individual enterprises. Understanding the strength of group effort, Lenz aggressively pursues partnerships with well-established nonprofits and companies.

To Lenz, being philanthropic goes beyond simply giving money or spreading awareness. It's about encouraging empathy and motivating people to take action. Often emphasizing the value of giving back, she exhorts her followers to identify topics they are passionate about and make a little personal contribution. She believes that everyone can contribute in some way, and that even modest efforts can have a positive knock-on effect. Lenz's approach to social media is clear evidence of her commitment to serving others. She uses her channels for more than just showcasing her next projects and posting pictures. She makes use of them to promote the work of organizations she supports, enlighten her followers about social challenges, and spark conversation about significant subjects. Lenz knows how to use social media as an activist tool, and she does so with skill to start discussions and motivate people to take action.

Bethany Joy Lenz

Lenz's charitable endeavors go beyond only supporting outside causes. She understands how critical it is to promote constructive change within the entertainment sector. She works to create a more equal and welcoming work environment and is a strong advocate for treating performers and crew members fairly. Bethany Lenz demonstrates her dedication to social justice beyond the stage by using her voice to combat prejudice and injustice in general society. Joy Lenz is an actor, but she's more than that. She is an inspiration who personifies the ability to use one's position for good. Her commitment to her charitable work, family, and faith encourages people to live compassionately and meaningfully. Lenz's unrelenting dedication to service, inventive partnerships, and ceaseless advocacy allow her to continue having a big effect on the globe.

Bethany Joy Lenz

CONCLUSION

We've followed Bethany Joy Lenz's fascinating journey in BETHANY JOY LENZ: EMBRACING CREATIVITY. She has demonstrated her ability to succeed in the competitive world of acting, the emotional world of music, and the developing field of directing. One thing has remained the same throughout it all: her unrelenting enthusiasm for artistic expression. This book was a masterwork in appreciating the complexity of creativity, not just a biography. Lenz's narrative challenged the notion that artistic pursuits should be confined within neat boundaries. Rather, it emphasized the value of pursuing many artistic interests and letting them influence and learn from one another. When you close this book, keep these Lenz tenets in mind:

Accept the unknowable: Don't be scared to venture into uncharted creative territory and leave your comfort zone. Discover your voice: Let your own viewpoint and life

Bethany Joy Lenz

experiences come through in whatever you do.

Work together with fervor. Be in the company of creative people who excite you similarly.

The key is balance: while commitment is necessary, give self-care first priority and learn constructive coping mechanisms for the demands of a creative life.

The narrative of Bethany Joy Lenz is far from finished. She will undoubtedly never stop surprising us with her stunning performances, heart-wrenching compositions, and daring directing ventures, thanks to her unyielding passion and limitless imagination. One thing is certain: for years to come, ambitious creatives will be motivated by the lessons they gain from their paths.

Thus, keep in mind Bethany Joy Lenz and her inspirational embrace of creation the next time you feel the need to create. Allow her story to serve as a prompt to discover your own special harmony and produce something exquisite.

The journey Bethany Joy Lenz takes in "Embracing Creativity" reveals the depth of her strength. Through the highs and lows of her artistic pursuits, she exemplifies

Bethany Joy Lenz

fortitude in the face of difficulties, bravery in pursuing novel ideas, and unshakable devotion to her art. By accepting vulnerability and authenticity, she fuels her creative expression, inspiring others to do the same. Bethany is the epitome of strength as she maneuvers through the challenges of creation; her power lies not just in her achievements but also in her courage and grace in facing her fears. She makes a lasting impression on her audience as well as the art world by embracing her creativity and realizing her own power while inspiring others to do the same.

Made in the USA
Columbia, SC
27 January 2025

198ac46c-ab51-4865-ad5a-e44227d41f9bR01